PAPER
SOULS

POETRY BY
JAROD WABICK

Copyright © 2020 by A.B.Baird Publishing

All rights reserved. This book or any portion thereof may not be reproduced or used in any manner whatsoever without the express written permission of the publisher except for the use of brief quotations in a book review.

Printed in the United States of America

First Printing, 2020

ISBN: 978-1-949321-15-9

All writings within this book belong to the author.

Cover Art & Design by: Austie M. Baird

A.B.Baird Publishing
66548 Highway 203
La Grande OR, 97850
USA

www.abbairdpublishing.com

Dedicated to those who take the time to read these words.
Thank you.

-Jarod Wabick

Table of Contents

Paper Soul

it seemed that
the more you
looked for your
soul

the more elusive
it
became

fluttering around
out there
in the wind
like a piece of aged
yellow newspaper

and even if you
managed
to
grab it out of the air

it was terribly difficult
not to
crumple it up
a bit

not to filthy it

with your

fingers

or grind a little

of it

to dust

The Hum of Panic

most mornings
i had long internal
monologues
with myself
about life
and all those great, important
questions
and after a coffee
or two
the monologue
sped up
faster, faster
faster
until it was just a low hum
and i would go out
and it would go on
humming and humming
until the night
when i fell back asleep
and then it would rest
and wait

Reaching

we wandered
about,
arms outstretched,
opening and
closing our fists

and most
times

we had no idea
what
we were reaching
for

Salt Water Bones

don't remember
when
but it
all
came crashing
in
like some great
wave

that i didn't
see
coming

and it washed
into
me

and the salt
water
is still lapping
up against
my
bones

while i try
to make
sense
of the silence

in a sea

of

noise

Gale Force

i could hear
the wind
battering the
world
loudly out-
side

and i wished
for it
to trounce down
the
walls

both those around
me

and

inside
me

Wail

swore i

heard

the sound of a coyote

howlin' out

into the night vapor

in the distance

or maybe

it was the wail

of a police siren

or an

ambulance

whatever it was

it shifted my soul

to hear it

this early in the morning

in the dark

in the cold

with the moon

hidin'

behind those thick

hazy

clouds

Front Porch

had room in
my chest
for
the world

the entire
goddamn
vile
thing

but it
just stood there

at the
door

hesitating

Beer

love and

beer

both softened

us

and then

made

us

tough as

nails

James Dean

we all knew
if we weren't paying close attention
the world would be the one
to break us
to destroy us
to leave us wrecked
in a gutter, blue-lipped
and lifeless
and this was all right,
for some - -
most, however,
wanted control
or at least something that seemed
like control
we wanted to be the ones to break us
so we drank or smoked
or drove fast on thin, dark
winding streets
or took all manners of drugs
and chances
and risks
and gambles
so that we could be the end of ourselves
to ensure that the world
doesn't get to us
first

Dead Weight

they never
taught us
that we would
need to
learn
how to let go

of so many
things

so that we
aren't lifting
lead limbs

out of bed
in the morning

Moved

i loved how truly

broken

and beaten

and damaged

we all could be

and still manage

somehow

to get up

and look each other

in the eyes

and say good

morning

Hang On

the strength

of our

grips

may

vary

but the

truth

is

we're all

just hanging

on

Old Empire

been coughing
up
soot &
smoke

as old
empires
crumble in-
side
me

while pillagers
rifle through
the art

in the
ruins

Naked

i stood in my room naked
after a shower hot enough
that i was confident
wore away
a layer of skin
and i didn't want
to get dressed
or dry off
or write
or speak
i didn't want to put on music,
or the tv
i didn't want to open the shades
to let the sun in
i didn't want to lie back down
or have a conversation
because it all felt so fabricated,
so phony
so i stood there
naked,
dripping water
on the floor
not sure
what to do
at all

Idol Hands

i was certain
that all the things
that every-
one
wanted

were simple
to
get

but a hundred
years or
so
is a long
while

so we make things
complicated

just to kill
some
time

Rewritten

life
was just a series
of short stories
interrupted by
sleep,
by alcohol,
by drugs and delirium,
by medication,
distractions,
by love and life
itself - -
life was just a series
of short stories
with poor character
development,
and lackluster
dialogue
stories that
could be
rewritten whenever
we wanted
if we only had
the nerve
to do so

Feng Shui

we all have
our own
hell

that we buy
furniture
for

hang art
in

add landscaping
to

and we make it
comfortable
and appealing

so that it
looks pretty
to the
world

Rise

it's in our
blood
to fight

something

to rise up
and against

something

and it seems
that this
thing

is usually

ourselves

Stories

i think our

greatest

fear

is no

one

listening

to our

story

or,

worse,

not

understanding

Killer

sometimes that
lump
crawls up
my throat

and my eyes start
to well
up

but i can push
it back down
and i cough to hide
it

and i'm still not sure
why

but i'm sure
it's another one of those things
that's killing
me

Man

i've swallowed
so many god-
damn
tears

because i feel
like i'm
not
allowed

that now
they've slumped
shoulders
sitting in
dark corner
bar room stools

wondering
why
they're so
unwanted

Grit

didn't dawn
on me

till the juke-
box
went quiet
and the
third beer
hit

to maybe try
dressing up
my fears

perhaps a suit &
tie,
maybe some wingtips
and some
cologne

maybe if they
liked
what they saw
in the
mirror

they'd have
a little more
grit

Genuine

my body
was no longer
held up by bones
but instead
by wrought iron bars
rusted and weathered
a chain-link cage
encased my lungs
and shielded my heart,
rubber tubing carried
blood
to all my leather organs,
brass hinges for joints
that creaked and moaned
and sometimes rusted over
and my smile seemed to be
the only part of me
that was still
genuine

Pretty Little Words

i was approached once
and told
that poetry was pointless
and all that it consisted of
was describing mundane things
with fancy words - -
"precisely"
i said
"precisely,...and sometimes
it even
hurts"

(De) Evolution

oh

what beautiful

creatures

we could be

until we woke up

and became

humans

Blood

after so many years
of not
bleeding

you start to forget
that there's blood
inside
you

pumping through
you

coursing through
you

and you start
to wonder

what is

Get Mad

when i was younger
i played little league baseball
and my dad would come to all my games
and before i would go up to bat
i'd look at him in the bleachers,
or a lawn chair
or leaned up against the fence
and he'd tell me "get mad"
he would say it out loud
or just mouth the words
"get mad"
with his right fist clenched
to fire me up
to get me to want it
to give me this slight vendetta
against the ball
against the pitcher
against the entire sport itself
"get mad" he would say
and i would grip the bat
so goddamn hard
that i could smell the wood burning in my palms
and i would stare at the pitcher
like a sworn enemy
and i would wait for the toss
and i don't think my dad
has any idea
that i still let those words
reverberate

over and over and over

in the back of my head

when i head out into the world every day

Wild

i often wondered
how beautiful
the world
would be

if we weren't
around

yelling and
fighting
and mashing our
feet
all over
it

Howl

i'm just
scared
that one
day

the moon
will be

so disappointed
in us

that it
won't

howl back

Daylight

unknotting and untangling
the sheets and comforter
from my legs,
shifting and sitting
on the side of the bed
stretching life back into my bones,
pushing life back into my eyes
focusing,
breathing a long exaggerated breath
that sometimes hurts the lungs,
placing my feet firmly on the carpet
gaining balance,
putting my fists up
squeezing them tight
relaxing them
and clenching again,
and walking out of the bedroom
door

Cosmonaut

we can

explore space

as much

as we want

but the

universe

sure as

hell

isn't going

to let

us

borrow another

planet

again

anytime

soon

Dismantle

up close

everything looks

like

a tiny, indecipherable

universe,

like art,

like something worth

writing about

like something worth

falling in love

with

and then,

over time,

those same things

start to look like something

worth dismantling

worth

destroying

Wretched

it reassured me
to know
that even the most
violent, heartless
and wretched beings
went to sleep at night

and were,
as it was,

completely vulnerable
and defenseless

just like
the rest of
us

Dead Art

sometimes i don't
feel bad
for humans
or humanity
at all

but, often times,
i find myself
feeling bad
for the art that ends up
on seedy motel
walls,

on gas station bathroom
walls,

stacked and stained
and torn
at garage sales,

forgotten in estate
sales

or lost forever
in the
trash

Humans

i kept quiet
and watched
and watched
& watched
and the animals acted
like animals
and the trees
acted like trees
the plants like plants
birds like birds
the stars did what stars do
the sun and moon
floated like gods
and the humans
acted like something
i could never really
recognize
or understand
or comprehend
or stomach
no matter how much
i watched
and watched
& watched

Such Sad Laughter

people lived such terribly
funny lives
in the way they acted
towards each other
and around each other

the way they acted
when they were alone
or thought they were
alone
or wanted to be
alone

they were funny in the way
they hurt each other
when they were scared
and how they were always scared
of being hurt

the way they tried to love
with their minds
and think
with their hearts - -

people were funny in the way
they tried to look
more alive
with potions and lotions
& elixirs

how they tried to appear younger
and act older

how they had so much to say
all the time
but said so very little

such funny lives
people lived

yet no one ever seemed
to laugh anymore

Gunfire

there used
to be
an honor and
code

to it
all

both good
or bad

now most
are just closing
their eyes
real tight

and firing shots
into the
darkness

Get There

so many
are so god-
damn
impatient
with their mad, frenzied
feverish
rush
to nowhere

with their
nowhere minds
and their
nowhere hearts
and their nowhere eyes
and their nowhere
anger

and they will
get there;

nowhere,

and they will
be elated

Sedatephobia

people make
noise
just to make
noise

because in the
silence

they fear
they might hear
their own
thoughts

and what their
souls
are really
trying
to
say

Prisms

we are

prisms

every one

of us

consuming our

individual

worlds

and violently

spilling

our colors

onto the

streets

trudging through

one another's

splashing through

one another's

drowning in

one another's

Dramatics

sex used to

sell

now drama

does

pain, suffering

embarrassment

the world

loves

to watch each-

other

fall

and

so

we

fall

Claws

we

were

all monsters

of some

sort

some of us

just had softer

claws

than others

Machinery

there's a
soot covered
soul

with a
shovel

in each and
every
skull

of the
quiet

throwing coal
in the
furnace

to keep
the machinery
running and
warm

and, although
the soul
with the shovel
is often
quiet,

the grinding
of the machinery
can be

deafening

Gray

everyone seems
so tired,
at least here;
on these
gray streets

tired with
life
tired with con-
versation
tired of doing
things they find
no pleasure
in

and i am exhausted
watching

watching the
luggage under their
eyes
fill and fill
and fill

exhausted with
watching the
smiling crows feet
fade and pull
towards

the dirt

the world just seems
so tired,
and i imagine they are
tired,
and i am
so very
tired

and we need rest
and we need
each other

Graffiti

there was a part
of town
dusty from crumbling
red brick
and cinder blocks
rich with art
in the form of graffiti
and dilapidation
a part of town
where every corner
housed a bar
or church
or liquor store
and people would filter
in and out of these establishments
at all hours
every day of the week
and it was always
for pretty much
the same exact
reason

Soul//Full

souls crash
into each other
every day,
sometimes so
loudly
the noise can be
unbearable

sometimes so
beautifully
the sight can be
intolerable

sometimes so tangibly
it can be felt
on the skin

the problem is
that no one
seems
to notice

or maybe
they just don't
care

Clouds

i watch as

airplanes cut through

the clouds

overhead

above everything

and i wonder

what stories

the passengers

have to tell,

want to tell,

need to tell,

struggle their entire lives

to tell

and i wonder

if anyone up there

is

happy

Piano Keys

everyone smiled on
with their false
smiles
all teeth
and piano keys
watering their tired eyes
and clearing their
tired throats
and they talked love
and talked hope
and talked of drugs,
booze and politics
and they talked of death
and ignored it
and talked of kindness
and ignored it
smiling on
all with just teeth
just jagged piano keys

Fifteen Cent Coffee

i knew the
journey
would be nothing
shy of strange
when i realized
how much i enjoyed
the fifteen cent
coffee
that sputtered lazily
into the styrofoam cup
from the vending machine
at the grocery store
i used to work at - -
because it takes a unique sort
to drink that sludge
and for an extra nickel
you could
even add cream

Settling Dust

i would come out
of all this
as someone
soot covered,
heart restored,
bones a bit whiter,
teeth a bit sharper,
tongue a bit softer,
and veins much tighter - -

i would come out
of all this
as someone - -

and i just hoped
it wasn't
as someone else

Violin Strings

i put on
the classical
station
because my mind
is a shattered
stained-glass window
of thought

and i just want
music - -
no words

and the violinist
takes hold
and it sounds
as though
the violin
is crying

and for a moment
i don't breathe
or blink
or worry

i just feel
and i just
feel sad
in the most peaceful way

and as the violin

weeps

i

am

free

Mourned

we were always mourning

something

or someone

until we were

finally

mourned ourselves

and that's why some

smiles

on some

faces

could bring a man

to his

knees

Light

life doesn't
change
all that much
over the
years

it just
burrow holes
in you

and then
the light
starts to filter
through
a little different

Static

i preferred
to listen to a radio
station
with a little
static

made it seem
just slightly more
genuine

because
as the station
filled
with more and more
static

i'd breathe
lighter

because this meant
i was getting
further away from
something

didn't matter
what it was

i was just headed
away

Curse the Earth

i glistened
with
sweat and
smelled of
beer
&
cheap cigar
smoke
and i

cursed the
earth
every now and
again

but the sun
never stopped
caressing my
skin

and the moon
never stopped
cradling my
bones

Cement Shoes

what a

shame

we can

float

but our

thoughts

weigh

us

down

Brawl

my organs
are just the
drunk and
rowdy
audience

to the back-
alley
fist-fight

between my
spirit
and my
soul

Love

drunk or
not

it takes
a lot

to let some-
one
disarm
you

to let some-
one

love
you

Arson

so many
seem to have
so little
soul
left

and maybe it's
scared or
maybe
we're scared

but when the
carpet catches fire
in the room
where it's
hiding

and it comes
bursting and flailing
all glowing and beaming
out the front
door

goddamn
what a
sight

Jet Black

that jet black
crow
inside me

that i wrote
about
years ago

he's still
there
resting on
a rib
where his claws
have left
little grooves
over time

and he rustles
his feathers
and
peers around
every so often

and he still
caws and
screeches
from time to time

but not as

much

as he used to

Butterfly//Bee

you get real
goddamn
good
at throwin'
punches
at yourself

then you start
learnin' how
to
duck

and that
can be
scary

Light//Dark

let 'em
love

the hell beneath
your finger-
tips

before they
go diggin'

for the heaven
buried in
your chest

Winter Poem

it got dark
and got
quiet
but it didn't get
that cold
for the time of season

which is
strange
here

and my mind
ran rampant
and fired off like
fireworks
but all the while
stayed in one
place

which is
strange
here

and the world

spun

and the people

yelled

and the animals

wept

but no music

played

which is

strange

here

Marble

i took the
world
out of my pocket

let it roll
around my
palm
like a marble

didn't want
to fight it today

just wanted to
stare at
it
for a bit

then i went
ahead

and put it
back

Bloodletting

as a kid
i left a lot of blood
on the street
outside my parents' house,
on the sidewalk,
the driveway,
the curbs & gutters,
in the woods out back,
the basement floor,
everywhere,
and it had been a couple decades
since i left any blood
anywhere
and i think that's the
problem

Asymmetrical

when it rained
particular parts of my soul
came crawling out
of all different caves and grottos
inside me
rubbing their eyes
and grinning asymmetrically
with that morning shine
on their cheekbones
the soft look
to their skin
before it wakes up
completely
and we would enjoy our time together

and when the sun came out
there were other parts
of my divided soul
that crept to the surface
and wrapped my bones
with their gentle claws
wincing against the daylight,
perching themselves
on the branches of trees
just behind
my eyes

Old Tobacco

while sitting
at a red light
the other day
i noticed an old timer
leaning on and slightly over
the bridge barrier
over cayuga creek
and he was tapping the bottom
of his pipe
cleaning out the old tobacco
and letting it fall into the rushing
water
and i saw his arms
adorned with military tattoos
from his watch
to the sleeve of his dickies shirt
and i wondered where he'd been,
what hell he'd been through
if any at all
and i decided for today
i wouldn't complain
about a goddamn thing

Death

i capsized a green bottle
of beer
down into my insides
and thought about
everyone that i loved
and had ever loved
and i waited for death
to pile his fat ass
through my front door
and when he did
i planned to put up
one hell
of a fight

Days End

the end of the world

came quick,

every night

and began again in the morning

waking you up,

nudging your lungs,

poking your heart with a stick

convincing you,

yet again,

to give it another go

for the billionth

time

Hands

i sometimes told my hands
that they would be okay
i felt i had to remind them

they seemed so far away at times
they were distant
and lonely
and they would grow weary
sometimes
and tired
always digging and digging
at my own insides
or another's
looking for answers, for hope
for solitude
and for another hand to hold
in the dirt and dust
and debris
i had to remind them
"it'll be ok" i'd say
just hold on

Revolution

the world had simply

not laughed

or loved

nearly enough

in the last billion years

and the muscles

in all our faces

had atrophied

and our hearts had

half-starved

and we all just seemed

ready

for a revolution

of benevolence

Drinking Buddies

i was drinking my morning coffee

when i saw an ant

scurrying across the counter

and i grabbed the

wall street journal,

and rolled it up,

instinctively,

ready to drive him into the countertop

but stopped

and realized he wasn't looking,

he had his back turned

and was crawling away

and that would make me

a coward

and so

i let him crawl up the business section

and i walked him outside

with a beer i grabbed

from the fridge

and i poured some on the back steps

and i let him inch off the paper

and into the pool

and we drank

together

Deafening

people are
becoming menacingly
and
belligerently
louder

with each
passing
day

and so must
the music

and so
must
the art

and so
must
the
love

Quicksand

poetry wasn't

understanding someone else's

hell

it was merely

recognizing the look

on their face

when they were

knee deep

in it

Nothing

i drank a cup of coffee
and read as much of the paper
as i could stomach
and read some poetry
and wrote some poetry
licked and sealed some envelopes
full of bills
and other nonsense
and walked them to the mailbox
on the corner
and it was still early
the world still quiet
and i wasn't quite sure what to do next
so i poured another cup
and sat there in silence
staring out the window
at nothing
at the same painting
and that was just fine
with me

Bad Times

it was a bad time for most things
or anything, really
for loving
or falling in love
for trying to find yourself
or others trying to find you
for genuine human emotion
expressed or otherwise
for pursuing dreams - -
real ones, the ones that buckle reality
for seeking truth
or being true to yourself
for being novel
or finding novel things
for creating, destroying, expanding
& elaborating
anything
for being a creature in this time
and this place - -
it was really just a bad time
for most things ·
or anything, really
and this
made it a pretty good time
for pretty much
everything

The Beat

i listened to record

after record

and stopped

drinking my beer

because i needed

a moment

i needed

room

for the beat

alongside

the one already in my chest

and the one

already in my head

and the beer

got warm

and my hands

got warm

and the whole room,

so empty and quiet,

started dancing

Blue Marble

i am

all at
once

a living, breathing
universe

encompassed and
engulfed
by a much larger
universe

one that i will
never
understand the purpose
of

and i am surrounded
by
a billion other

universes

all clashing
and colliding
and trying
to
coexist

Birdsong

the birds
were the first song
i would hear
in the morning - -
singing their melodies,
perched high
on the power lines outside
watching over me
and i was scared
of disappointing
them
more than
anything else

Grime

created sloppy,

sticky,

bar-floor

art

to try and

convince

the

universe

that even though

we are

disgusting,

appalling

creatures

sometimes

our minds

are

not

Vagabonds

when i was younger
someone once taught me
to always blow kisses
when driving under bridges
with trains crossing
above
and you would do this
to send your love
and luck
and warm goodbyes
to those holed up
in graffitied
boxcars,
those vagabonds
and drifters
on the lamb
running away from,
and sometimes even
towards,
something

Long Road

we pick
a few people
to join us
for the
ride

to help
convince us
that we'll
never
die

then we watch
each
other
fall apart

as attractively
as
we
can

Laughter

what madness

when i
learned

that the hand
around my
throat
was my own

what
humor

what cosmic
laughter

Glow

your glow
isn't gone
kid

it's just
covered in
dust

from the
crumbling of
humanity

Resiliency

my body
knew better
than to
give in

knew it had
my mind
to worry
about

and the entire
world
inside it

Window Pains

we are

all

knocking on

the windows

from the inside

of our

own

little worlds

and

waiting

to see if any-

one

hears

and decides

to look

in

Art

eventually

life makes

artists

of us

all

until we're

buried

as the

finished

piece of art

that we

never

really realized

we'd been

working on

in the first

place

Stitch

there have
been moments

where i have been
able
to tighten and restitch
the seams
where they have
started to
tear

and i used
different color
threads
with different
textures
and
different strengths

and this eclectic
woven
soul

that clings to me
tightly

is more me
than it has
even been

Erosion

the world isn't
wearing
you
down
it's just grinding
away
all those parts
that are hiding
the human
inside you

Dizzy

awake

from that
dizzy,
sleepy
state
and

arrange your
bones
how you would
like
and just

keep swingin'
those
flower-petal
fists

Vision

you have to
stop looking for
beauty

with your
eyes

it's the only
goddamn
sense

that doesn't
have
any

Etched

you don't have
to tell
me

what the
world
did to you

if you don't want
to

but what
are you going
to do

with all the
beautiful
art

that it
left
on your
bones

Dancing

we shouldn't
be carrying
as much of the world
as we do

but we
do

and in the end
and even before then
it makes us
stronger
not
weaker

and the trembling
& shaking
of our legs
beneath it
all

let's just
consider it
dancing

Imperfect Galaxies

there are no
humans

just galaxies
with limbs

with lungs
and
livers

with skin

pulled tight
or pulling
towards the
ground

always imperfect
and
always

beautiful

Fragile

what truly
makes us
strong

is accepting
that we
are

fragile

Flowers

beneath the
pollution
of gunfire &
smoke

are
flowers

always

Rain//Gutter

three decades
of rain

and
i

still stared
out the
window
at it

like it was
some great
mystical
happening

and when i'd
finally
turn away

i'd feel as
though
some vacant
space
in my body

had been
filled
just slightly

Ink

some people
got irritated
if you wrote too literal,
too concrete
and didn't use enough symbolism
or imagery - -
other people got mad
if you used too many
metaphors
or cliché's
or got too romantic
or too idealistic
or too tender & amorous
and compared love to too many
things
or compared pain to too many
things
but always be wary
of those who are maddened
if you write
absolutely anything
at all

Powerlines

there were

wealthier parts of town

where they had buried

the telephone wires

beneath the

dirt

beneath the earth

and there was nowhere

for the birds to land

to perch

to rest and

watch over everything

and i felt sorry

for the people

in these

parts

Selfish

i simply wanted to lie there
in the valley in the middle of my bed
that had formed over the years
and i wanted to ponder unimportant things,
ghastly things,
beautifully tragic things
and terribly wondrous things
and i didn't want to write them down
or type them out
i wanted to selfishly keep them
for myself
all my peculiar little thoughts
and i would smile
and sigh, heavily;
roll out of the valley
and get up
and finally
go about
my day
with this watercolor painting
that's caught in a rainstorm
swirling around my head

Rocking Chair

even if you
have to nail all
your furniture
to the
ceiling

every now and
then
try to look
at the world
differently

from a different
point of
view

it just might
save your
life

or maybe
someone
else's

Masks

we are not
wearing masks

we are just
often
unsure
which color of
iris
to wear
on any given
day

unsure how sharp
of a tongue
to bring
along

how hard or
soft
to clench our
fists

how loud to prepare
our lungs
and
voice
to be

unsure of how

cunning

to allow our wit

to be,

our sarcasm,

our humor,

our

rage

unsure of when

to smile and

when

to bare our teeth indignantly

when to bare them

threateningly

we are not

wearing masks

we just have trouble

figuring out

who to be

on any given

day

True Beauty

the beauty of
the world
is rarely in
the world
itself

but, instead,

how it spills
and splashes

off the eyes
and skin
and lips

of the being
sitting across
from
you

Barstool Saints

i have seen more saints

on street corners

and more gods

on barstools

than i imagined

i would ever see

in the clouds

i was able to buy them beers

and watch them smile

and shake their

hands

and feel the rough

grit

of their working palms

and i could see years

of fight

in their weary eyes

and i knew they had their stories

of struggle and triumph

stories of tougher times

stories that they may never

tell

the sort of stories

that no god

could ever match

Landlord

the devil
may be
the landlord

but decorate
the place
however the hell
you want

tear up the cigarette burned
carpets
and
polish the hardwood
floors

pound large nails
into the
walls
and hang art;

loud, colorful, vibrant
blinding, eccentric
art

knock down those choking
claustrophobic walls
and
open the place
up

play loud music
past the curfew
of the
noise ordinance

the devil
may be
the landlord

but raise hell
while you're
the tenant

Ghost

if you can't convince
your ghosts
to go to sleep
set them free
to roam about
and slip in and out
of strangers eyes
and strangers lungs
and strangers lips
let them see
what the real world is like
outside of your chest
outside of your skull
outside of your
heart
where they have fed
on your fire for years - -
if you can't convince
your ghosts
to go to sleep
set them free
let them tire out
let them exhaust themselves
entirely
and go hungry
and go thirsty
and let them evaporate
and die

Milestones

we celebrated events
that were trivial at best
because we needed
something to be excited about,
to cheer about,
to gather and drink and laugh
about
we needed small landmarks
to feel like we were accomplishing
something,
moving forward, progressing

we created small milestones
and treated them like miracles
or historic spectacles - -

and this was all ok
because we sure as hell
needed it

Flimsy Little Vessels

i knew
better
we all knew better
that's really all life
was
just a series of lessons
learned and ignored
because sometimes we touched
the stove
even after we were burned
and sometimes we poked
the sleeping beast
even after we'd been bitten
and sometimes we sailed out to sea
in our flimsy little vessels
even after we were capsized
tossed around
and beat against the reef
because we were stubborn
and hardheaded
because we were human
and flawed and inconsistent
and we knew that love
didn't often play by the rules
so we often wondered,
why should we?

Fighter

if this
fight

against my-
self
is

inevitable

you can be
sure as
hell

i'm going
to
win

Be

be so fascinating

and interesting,

wild and crazed

and furious

and loving

that death gets caught up

watching

and forgets to do his

job

Pint

regardless of hell
sipping a beer
on my front
steps

it was still
beautiful
to wake up

still beautiful
to breathe

still beautiful
to
exist

still beautiful
to pour a
pint
and sit
right down there
on the steps
next to him

Space

as the
world got darker
we held each other
tighter
and i knew
when we finally
got to hell
there wouldn't be
the slightest
bit of space
between us

Gentle Steps

i wondered
for quite some
time

if, maybe,
my gentle steps
on the earth

could be felt
as soft vibrations
on the soles
of the feet
of those on the
opposite side
of the world

and i am comforted
in maintaining the
belief

that they
could

Family

we drank decent beer,
not the worst,
but certainly not the best
and it rained and rained
and rained
and we listened to a recording
that someone bought
of what outer-space sounds like
when radio waves are shot up there
which i imagine was done
for scientific reasons
and we discussed misanthropy
and futility,
natural disasters, chaos and upheaval
and we laughed
and talked and sang
and we solved the world's problems
and someone quoted Che
while someone quoted Lennon
laughing ourselves into exhaustion
while space went on
moaning and echoing
somewhere vast and dark
and peaceful

Dispersal

i only want
a few slivers
of my soul
left

when i take
it
to my
grave

and the rest
scattered
in all those
places

where i have
opened up
and left
it

Star Gazer

my mind is
dark

so i look
for

the light

in
others

Saints

there are

no

saints

only people

trying

to be better

because we all

have a

darkness

that we

deny

or fight

or co-

exist

with

a darkness

we can learn

from

if only we

acknowledge

its existence

Ache

ache with
me

ache entirely

eaten up
by it
and chewed
and consumed
and ground up
by it

ache in each
and
every
bone

and every
muscle

and in every
chamber
of the
heart

let the ache
scream and sing
and laugh
and cry and stumble

and trip
and stagger to its
feet

always ache
with every
emotion

ache entirely

never hide
them

and ache with
me

War Heroes

i always preferred
secondhand bookstores
to the opposite, - -

they always had
such character
and smelled differently
and felt differently

they had a feel of warmth
and worn love

and there was an overall
feeling of post-war relief
that all these books
had survived unknowable hells
and unspeakable tragedies
and now rested on a shelf,
quietly

all tattered with wounded
spines
and torn insides
splattered with ink
that wasn't their own

wearing their scars
proudly
with a dignified

and humble

tenacity

Bloody Knuckles

i don't have
to see
your
bloody knuckles
or

your split
lip

to know
that you're
a

fighter

i can see it
in

your smile

Drapes

people seemed
most beautiful to
me

when their walls
turned to
drapes
and fell to the
floor

when their heads
tilted
ever so slightly
to the side
and they muscle
a smile

and their labored
lives
came spilling out
the corners of
their
mouths

Balance

the body
and the mind
need
to experience
a wide array
of drastic and
overwhelming
emotions

in order to
stay
balanced

you do not
need to
be

happy

all of the
time

Sight

maybe it was never

about the madman

or the sane man

the crooks or the cops

or the gods or the liars

the rich

the paupers

the fighters

or the doves

maybe it wasn't about the monks

or the murderers

or the priests or the non-believers

maybe it was just about having

your eyes open

at the right time

in the right place

and seeing things

for exactly

what they are

Too Much//Too Little

when you are
a child
and untethered

you know very
little

and it is
perfect

and when you
are old
and nearing your
death

you know too
much

and it is
perfect

Soul

maybe no
god

but soul;
always
soul

raging,
passionate soul

roarin' and
singin'
and wailin'

for anything
and
everything

in case

if in the
end

there is
nothing

Belief

i've nothing
against
your
god

or any
god

I'm just saying
please
believe

in your-
self

first

Hard Hearts

all these hard writers
with their hard hearts
and hard words, and
hard poetry,
hardened bones
from a hardened past
all sat
at some point
in a dark dark room
with syrupy eyes
all glazed and crystalline
having loved, finally
having loved, after all

Beneath

there are very few
truths
left
but they are there
buried under debris
under ruins
of old cities
and new cities
under business suits
and sunday's-best
under medications
under drugs
and sunglasses and plastic
surgery
buried under make-up
and facades
covered in pretense
and expensive,
useless words - -

there are very few truths
but they are there;
i can
promise you - -

because if they are not
we have been fighting
a very hard battle
for a very long time
for really no reason
at all

Ashes//Dust

i don't want my bones
to be found,
dug up or unearthed,
i want them crushed
and turned to dust
in some nameless town
on some nameless road
where the angry winds
can carry me
to the sunny, jagged
side
of some nameless
mountain

Runneth Over

it happened more
now
than it ever
had in the
past

catching my
soul
pouring out
of my body

pouring out
of me

out over my
shoes

and into the
dirt

and into
the clay

it kept
happening

and i never seemed
to run
out

Bully

bullied my
body
and
cursed my
skin

for
years

but, today,
outside
with the sun
and
breeze

and only the clouds
listening

i apologized to
and thanked
every inch
of myself
for its
resiliency

Honest Earth

the earth never complained
like we did
never put on masks
like we did
it never tried to be anything other
than exactly what it was
like we so often did
the earth just lay there
quietly; waiting to be written
waiting to be understood
swaying in the wind
just waiting to be loved
to be touched
to be cared for, caressed
& believed
for all of its secrets
and all of its obscurities
and it wanted all of this
without judgement
without prejudice
just simple, unconditional
compassion

Sway

it's all
just one long
dance

that we learn
the steps
to
along the
way

and it hurts
because we're
using new
muscles
with each new
day

and it hurts
because we start
to attach emotion
to the
music

and it hurts
because it's all
about
holding on

and it's beautiful
because of
all of
this

Unapologetic

i am laughing
long, hard
belly laughs

i am drinking
good beer
and
shitty beer

i am watching
the world

and i am
listening

i am taking
up
cosmic space

and i am not
apologizing

Persistent

i will spill a poem
one day
that will bring my family
to tears
my friends
to tears
neighbors, strangers
and enemies
to absolute tears
it will snatch the air
from the lungs of birds
and the air from beneath
their wings
and they will plummet
violently
to the ground
and i won't have written
a single
word

Jarod Wabick was born in Las Vegas, NY and moved to Buffalo, NY when he was 5. Wabick, who has always lived in the dreamland of a writer's mind, finds grounding in the everyday nuances of life in his suburban world. The never ending drone of life - planes screaming overhead, sirens emanating from a distance, lawnmowers grumbling, and birds singing above it all — give way to countless moments of reflection and inspiration. Wabick believes that he found his true voice in a typewriter that was stumbled upon at an antique shop in his early 20's. The arts have become Wabick's release as he enjoys reading poetry, feeling art and listening to a wide array of music while allowing himself to simply ride the waves of each moment. Wabick also enjoys down time investing in discovering the joys of beer, wine, whiskey, and bird-watching (while indulging in said libations).

Want to find more work by Jarod Wabick?

You can find his works published in:

"Like Frost on the Winter Garden" available on Amazon
"Crown Anthology" available on Amazon

Or find him on social media at:

Instagram
@rodandrew16